I CHOOSE YOU

YOU
(EVERY DAY & ALWAYS)

WRITTEN BY
DANIELLE LEDUC MCQUEEN

ILLUSTRATED BY
YUMI SAKUGAWA

I CHOOSE YOU.
GIVEN EVERY
OPPORTUNITY,
I'LL ALWAYS
CHOOSE YOU.

THERE ARE BILLIONS OF PEOPLE ON THIS PLANET AND ONE TRILLION WAYS TO FIND LOVE.

BUT WHAT
WE HAVE
IS SOMETHING
EXTRAORDINARY.

WHAT WE HAVE WE
CHOOSE, WE FORGE IT
FROM THE ENDLESS
LITTLE MOMENTS WE
SQUEEZE OUT OF
EVERY DAY.

I CHOOSE YOU EVERY
MORNING BECAUSE
OUR CONNECTION IS
SOMETHING THAT
WE'RE ALWAYS
CREATING.

IT'S IN THE MEALS WE
COOK, THE WORDS WE
USE, AND THE INSTANT
WE LOOK UP AND
LISTEN.

THE EFFORT COMES
NATURALLY, THE CHOICE
SO SIMPLY, BECAUSE
I KNOW THAT ALL I NEED
TO BE HAPPY IS

MY PARTNER,

MY TRUE FRIEND,

MY ALLY IN

ALL THINGS: YOU.

OUR BOND IS STICKY AND UNSHAKABLE. EVEN THROUGH THE HARD STUFF AND THE DAYS

WE SHARE A STORY,
A LANGUAGE, AND
A WAY OF SEEING.

WE SHARE A BEAUTIFUL
WORLD ALL OUR OWN.

BUT OUR MAGIC BUBBLE ONLY EXISTS BECAUSE WE TEND TO IT,

BECAUSE WE GIVE IT WHAT IT NEEDS TO FLOURISH:

HONEST CONVERSATIONS,

NEVER-ENDING TRUST,

A GROUNDSWELL
OF RESPECT,

AND, ABOVE ALL,
OUR THOUGHTFUL
AND DEDICATED TIME.

TOGETHER WE'RE CHOOSING TO OPEN OUR HEARTS,

TO PAUSE AND APPRECIATE, TO EMPATHIZE AND CONNECT.

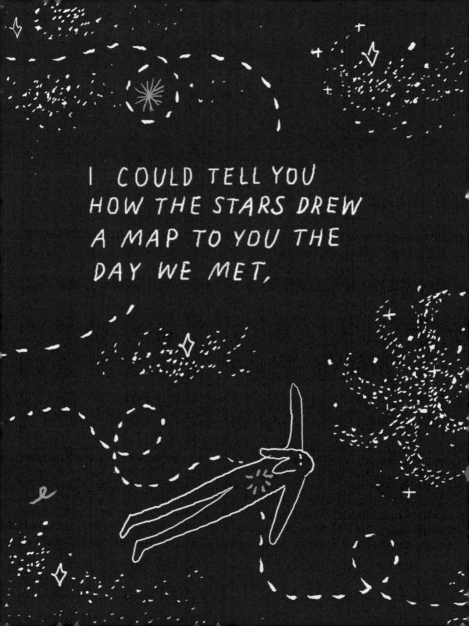

OR TRY TO
DESCRIBE HOW YOU'RE
THE MESMERIZING
SUPERNOVA AT THE
CENTER OF MY
UNIVERSE.

I COULD TELL YOU THAT
WE'RE MEANT TO BE
BECAUSE OF HOW THE WORLD
SPARKLES IN YOUR EYES

AND HOW
YOUR SILLY LITTLE JOKES
MAKE ME GIGGLE.

BUT THAT'S NOT
THE MIRACLE
OF OUR LOVE.

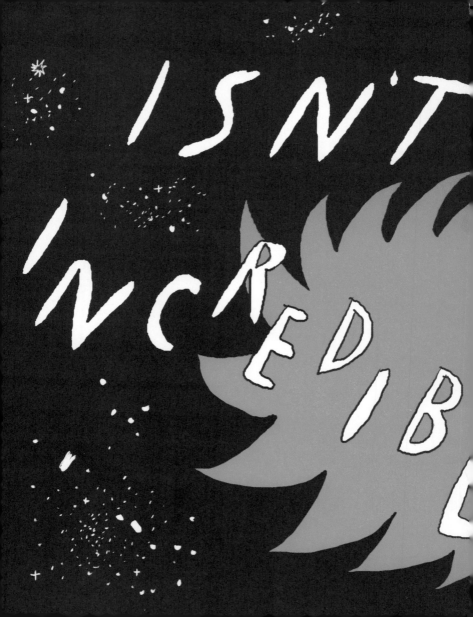

TIME AND
CIRCUMSTANCE
WILL CHANGE
WHO WE ARE,

BUT OUR LOVE
WILL GROW AS
WE CHANGE
AND CHANGE AS
WE GROW.

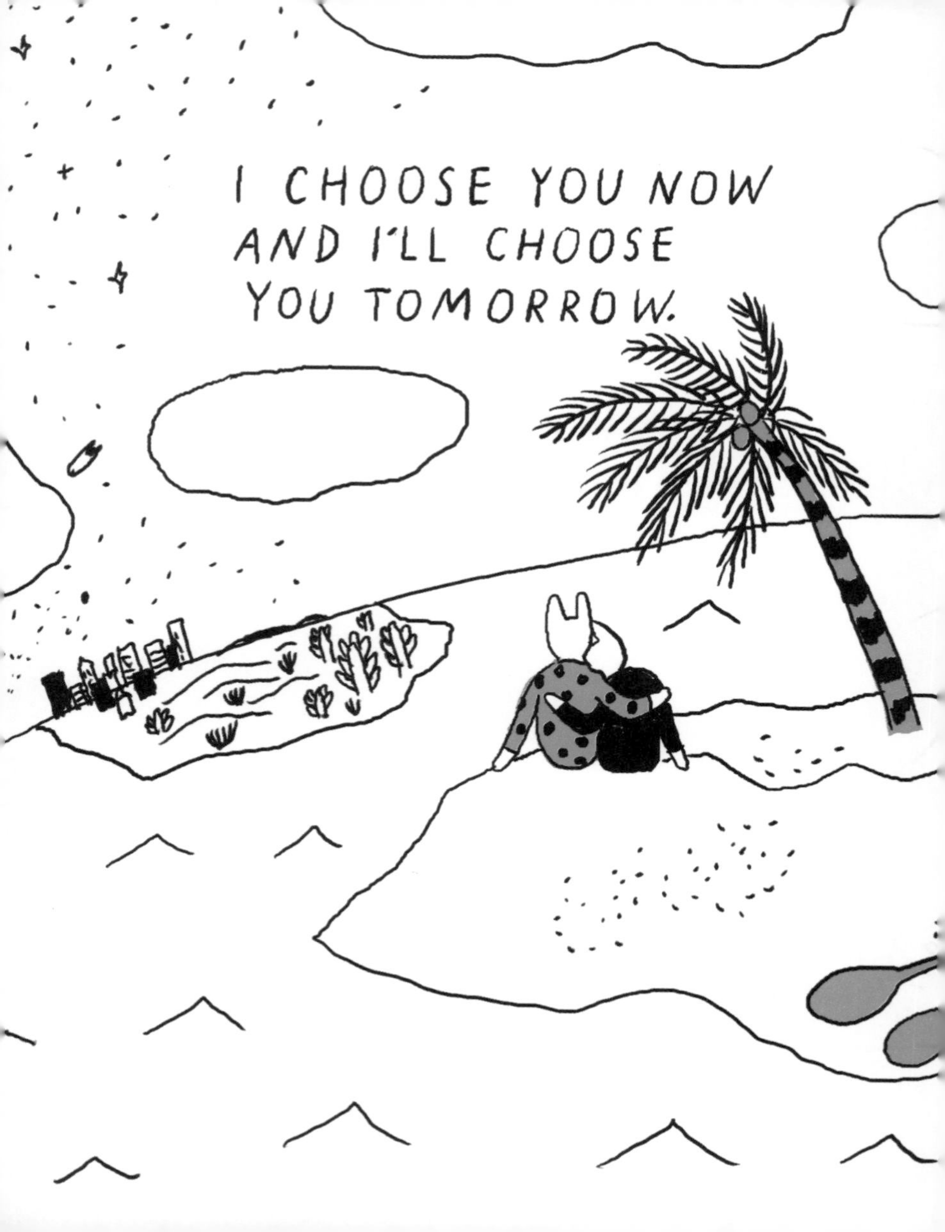
I CHOOSE YOU NOW
AND I'LL CHOOSE
YOU TOMORROW.

COMPENDIUM.
live inspired

WRITTEN BY: DANIELLE LEDUC MCQUEEN
ILLUSTRATED BY: YUMI SAKUGAWA
EDITED BY: RUTH AUSTIN
ART DIRECTED BY: SARAH FORSTER

Library of Congress Control Number: 2017958716 | ISBN: 978-1-946873-02-6

5th printing. Printed in China with soy inks on FSC®-Mix certified paper.

Create meaningful moments with gifts that inspire.

CONNECT WITH US
live-inspired.com | sayhello@compendiuminc.com

@compendiumliveinspired
#compendiumliveinspired